Chapter one:

Origins of Irish surnames

According to an old saying, there are two types of Irish – those who actually are Irish and those who wish they were.

This sentiment is only one example of the allure that the high romance and drama of the proud nation's history holds for thousands of people scattered across the world today.

It's a sad fact, however, that the vast majority of Irish surnames are found far beyond Irish shores, rather than on the Emerald Isle itself.

The population stood at around eight million souls in 1841, but today it stands at fewer than six million.

This is mainly a tragic consequence of the potato famine, also known as the Great Hunger, which devastated Ireland between 1845 and 1849.

The Irish peasantry had become almost wholly reliant for basic sustenance on the potato, first introduced from the Americas in the seventeenth century.

When the crop was hit by a blight, at least 800,000 people starved to death while an estimated two million others were forced to seek a new life far from their native shores – particularly in America, Canada, and Australia.

The effects of the potato blight continued until about 1851, by which time a firm pattern of emigration had become established.

Ireland's loss, however, was to the gain of the countries in which the immigrants settled, contributing enormously, as their descendants do today, to the well being of the nations in which their forefathers settled.

But those who were forced through dire circumstance to establish a new life in foreign parts never forgot their roots, or the proud heritage and traditions of the land that gave them birth.

Nor do their descendants.

It is a heritage that is inextricably bound up in the colourful variety of Irish names themselves – and the origin and history of these names forms an integral part of the vibrant drama that is the nation's history, one of both glorious fortune and tragic misfortune.

This history is well documented, and one of the most important and fascinating of the earliest sources are *The Annals of the Four Masters*, compiled between 1632 and 1636 by four friars at the Franciscan Monastery in County Donegal.

Compiled from earlier sources, and purporting to go back to the Biblical Deluge, much of the material takes in the mythological origins and history of Ireland and the Irish.

This includes tales of successive waves of invaders and settlers such as the Fomorians, the Partholonians, the Nemedians, the Fir Bolgs, the Tuatha De Danann, and the Laigain.

Of particular interest are the *Milesian Genealogies*,

McKenna

by Iain Gray

Lang**Syne**

PUBLISHING

WRITING *to* REMEMBER

WRITING *to* REMEMBER

E-mail: info@lang-syne.co.uk

Distributed in the Republic of Ireland by Portfolio Group,
Kilbarrack Ind. Est. Kilbarrack, Dublin 5.
T:00353(01) 839 4918 F:00353(01) 839 5826
sales@portfoliogroup.ie
www.portfoliogroup.ie

Design by Dorothy Meikle   Printed by Fixture Displays, China

ISBN 978-1-85217-304-3

McKenna

MOTTO:
Roll of flax to victory.

CREST:
A salmon.

NAME variations include:
Mac Cionaoda *(Gaelic)*
Mac Cinna *(Gaelic)*
Mac Cionnaith *(Gaelic)*
Mac Cionath *(Gaelic)*
MacKenna
MacKennagh
MacKenney
MacKinna
MacKinnie

because the majority of Irish clans today claim a descent from either Heremon, Ir, or Heber – three of the sons of Milesius, a king of what is now modern day Spain.

These sons invaded Ireland in the second millennium B.C, apparently in fulfilment of a mysterious prophecy received by their father.

This Milesian lineage is said to have ruled Ireland for nearly 3,000 years, until the island came under the sway of England's King Henry II in 1171 following what is known as the Cambro-Norman invasion.

This is an important date not only in Irish history in general, but for the effect the invasion subsequently had for Irish surnames.

'Cambro' comes from the Welsh, and 'Cambro-Norman' describes those Welsh knights of Norman origin who invaded Ireland.

But they were invaders who stayed, inter-marrying with the native Irish population and founding their own proud dynasties that bore Cambro-Norman names such as Archer, Barbour, Brannagh, Fitzgerald, Fitzgibbon, Fleming, Joyce, Plunkett, and Walsh – to name only a few.

These 'Cambro-Norman' surnames that still flourish throughout the world today form one of the three main categories in which Irish names can be placed – those of Gaelic-Irish, Cambro-Norman, and Anglo-Irish.

Previous to the Cambro-Norman invasion of the twelfth century, and throughout the earlier invasions and settlement of those wild bands of sea rovers known as the Vikings in the eighth and ninth centuries, the population of the island was relatively small, and it was normal for a person to be identified through the use of only a forename.

But as population gradually increased and there were many more people with the same forename, surnames were adopted to distinguish one person, or one community, from another.

Individuals identified themselves with their own particular tribe, or 'tuath', and this tribe – that also became known as a clann, or clan – took its name from some distinguished ancestor who had founded the clan.

The Gaelic-Irish form of the name Kelly, for example, is Ó Ceallaigh, or O'Kelly, indicating descent from an original 'Ceallaigh', with the 'O' denoting 'grandson of.' The name was later anglicised to Kelly.

The prefix 'Mac' or 'Mc', meanwhile, as with the clans of the Scottish Highlands, denotes 'son of.'

Although the Irish clans had much in common with their Scottish counterparts, one important difference lies in what are known as 'septs', or branches, of the clan.

Septs of Scottish clans were groups who often bore an entirely different name from the clan name but were under the clan's protection.

In Ireland, septs were groups that shared the same name and who could be found scattered throughout the four provinces of Ulster, Leinster, Munster, and Connacht.

The 'golden age' of the Gaelic-Irish clans, infused as their veins were with the blood of Celts, pre-dates the Viking invasions of the eighth and ninth centuries and the Norman invasion of the twelfth century, and the sacred heart of the country was the Hill of Tara, near the River Boyne, in County Meath.

Known in Gaelic as 'Teamhar na Rí', or Hill of Kings, it was the royal seat of the 'Ard Rí Éireann', or High King of Ireland, to whom the petty kings, or chieftains, from the island's provinces were ultimately subordinate.

It was on the Hill of Tara, beside a stone pillar known as the Irish 'Lia Fáil', or Stone of Destiny, that the High Kings were inaugurated and, according to legend, this stone would emit a piercing screech that could be heard all over Ireland when touched by the hand of the rightful king.

The Hill of Tara is today one of the island's main tourist attractions.

Opposition to English rule over Ireland, established in the wake of the Cambro-Norman invasion, broke out frequently and the harsh solution adopted by the powerful forces of the Crown was to forcibly evict the native Irish from their lands.

These lands were then granted to Protestant colonists, or 'planters', from Britain.

Many of these colonists, ironically, came from Scotland and were the descendants of the original 'Scotti', or 'Scots', who gave their name to Scotland after migrating there in the fifth century A.D., from the north of Ireland.

Colonisation entailed harsh penal laws being imposed on the majority of the native Irish population, stripping them practically of all of their rights.

The Crown's main bastion in Ireland was Dublin and its environs, known as the Pale, and it was the dispossessed peasantry who lived outside this Pale, desperately striving to eke out a meagre living.

It was this that gave rise to the modern-day expression of someone or something being 'beyond the pale'.

Attempts were made to stamp out all aspects of the ancient Gaelic-Irish culture, to the extent that even to bear a Gaelic-Irish name was to invite discrimination.

This is why many Gaelic-Irish names were anglicised with, for example, and noted above, Ó Ceallaigh, or O'Kelly, being anglicised to Kelly.

Succeeding centuries have seen strong revivals of Gaelic-Irish consciousness, however, and this has led to many families reverting back to the original form of their name, while the language itself is frequently found on the fluent tongues of an estimated 90,000 to 145,000 of the island's population.

Ireland's turbulent history of religious and political strife is one that lasted well into the twentieth century, a landmark century that saw the partition of the island into the twenty-six counties of the independent Republic of

Ireland, or Eire, and the six counties of Northern Ireland, or Ulster.

Dublin, originally founded by Vikings, is now a vibrant and truly cosmopolitan city while the proud city of Belfast is one of the jewels in the crown of Ulster.

It was Saint Patrick who first brought the light of Christianity to Ireland in the fifth century A.D.

Interpretations of this Christian message have varied over the centuries, often leading to bitter sectarian conflict – but the many intricately sculpted Celtic Crosses found all over the island are symbolic of a unity that crosses the sectarian divide.

It is an image that fuses the 'old gods' of the Celts with Christianity.

All the signs from the early years of this new millennium indicate that sectarian strife may soon become a thing of the past – with the Irish and their many kinsfolk across the world, be they Protestant or Catholic, finding common purpose in the rich tapestry of their shared heritage.

Chapter two:

Sons of the dirk

An area known as Emyvale in the north of present day Co. Monaghan was for centuries the homeland of bearers of the proud name of McKenna.

An explanation of how they came to settle there in about the eighth century A.D. can be found on the clan's coat of arms – that features the figure of a hunter on horseback, his two hounds, a stag, and two crescent moons.

The crescent moons are symbolic of the two days and nights that a McKenna chieftain from the area of Kells, in present day Co. Meath, had spent in pursuit of the stag.

He and his faithful hounds finally ran it to bay at what is now Liskenna, in Emyvale.

It was here that he plunged his dagger, or dirk, into the beast's heart – and this may well provide an explanation for the McKenna motto of 'sons of the dirk', while their motto of 'Roll of flax to victory' is thought to derive from the cockade of flax that their warriors wore into battle.

Exhausted after his long and arduous expedition, the McKenna hunter gratefully accepted the hospitality of a local chieftain known as Treanor – who was so impressed with the young man's hunting skills and charm that he offered him his daughter's hand in marriage.

After several weeks of enjoying the hospitality of

Treanor and the bridal charms of his daughter, the McKenna chieftain received word that his own kingdom had been usurped in his absence by rival kinsfolk.

Rather than travelling back to his former kingdom with his young bride, he decided to settle in Emyvale – becoming the founder of a dynasty of McKennas that would rule for centuries as the Lords of Truagh, in what was a territory of roughly eighty square miles.

The clan's headquarters were established at Tully, near Liskenna, and it was here that they built an imposing series of ring forts atop a hill while a fortification was also erected in the middle of a nearby lake.

The name Liskenna, meanwhile, the original scene of the McKenna hunter's triumph over the stag, derives its name from the Gaelic 'Lios Sceine', indicating 'the fort of the knife.'

To the south of the McKenna territory lay the homeland of the McMahons, while to the north lay the territories of the powerful O'Neills.

While not fighting among themselves for control of the lordship of Truagh, the McKennas were also frequently at war with the O'Neills and the McMahons – much in the same manner that their Celtic counterparts in the Highlands and Islands of Scotland were also often engaged in destructive warfare with one another.

It was this disunity that was to ultimately lead to disastrous consequences for the native Irish clans such as the McKennas, as invaders from foreign shores exploited it to their advantage.

This was illustrated to dramatic and tragic effect in the late twelfth century.

By 1156 the most powerful of Ireland's kings was Muirchertach MacLochlainn, king of the McKenna neighbours, the O'Neills.

The equally powerful Rory O'Connor, king of the province of Connacht, opposed him but he increased his power and influence by allying himself with Dermot MacMurrough, king of Leinster.

MacLochlainn and MacMurrough were aware that the main key to the kingdom of Ireland was the thriving trading port of Dublin that had been established by invading Vikings, or Ostmen, in 852A.D.

Their combined forces took Dublin, but when MacLochlainn died the Dubliners rose up in revolt and overthrew the unpopular MacMurrough.

A triumphant Rory O'Connor entered Dublin and was later inaugurated as Ard Rí, but MacMurrough refused to accept defeat.

He appealed for help from England's Henry II in unseating O'Connor, an act that was to radically affect the future course of Ireland's fortunes.

The English monarch agreed to help MacMurrough, but distanced himself from direct action by delegating his Norman subjects in Wales with the task.

These ambitious and battle-hardened barons and knights had first settled in Wales following the Norman Conquest of England in 1066 and, with an eye on rich booty, plunder, and lands, were only too eager to obey their sovereign's wishes and furnish MacMurrough with aid.

He crossed the Irish Sea to Bristol, where he rallied powerful barons such as Robert Fitzstephen and Maurice Fitzgerald to his cause, along with Gilbert de Clare, Earl of Pembroke.

The mighty Norman war machine soon moved into action, and so fierce and disciplined was their onslaught on the forces of O'Connor and his allies that by 1170 they had re-captured Dublin, in the name of MacMurrough, and other strategically important territories.

Henry II now began to take cold feet over the venture, realising that he may have created a rival in the form of a separate Norman kingdom in Ireland.

Accordingly, he landed on the island, near Waterford, at the head of a large army in October of 1171 with the aim of curbing the power of his Cambro-Norman barons.

But protracted war between the king and his barons was averted when they submitted to the royal will, promising homage and allegiance in return for holding the territories they had conquered in the king's name.

Henry also received the submission and homage of many of the Irish chieftains, tired as they were with internecine warfare and also perhaps realising that as long as they were rivals and not united they were no match for the powerful forces the English Crown could muster.

English dominion over Ireland was ratified through the Treaty of Windsor of 1175, under the terms of which Rory O'Connor, for example, was allowed to rule territory unoccupied by the Normans in the role of a vassal of the king.

Two years earlier, Pope Alexander III had given Papal sanction to Henry's dominance over Ireland, on condition that he uphold the rights of the Holy Roman Catholic Church and that chieftains adhere rigorously to the oaths of fealty they had sworn to the English king.

While many Irish clans were reluctantly forced to seek an accommodation with the English Crown, others took a defiant stance of resistance – not least clans such as the McKennas and the O'Neills, who now found themselves belatedly united in the face of a common foe.

One indication of the harsh conditions under which they suffered, as the English Crown's grip on the island tightened like a noose around their necks, can be found in a desperate plea sent to Pope John XII by Roderick O'Carroll of Ely, the McKenna ally Donald O'Neill of Ulster, and a number of other Irish chieftains in 1318.

They stated: 'As it very constantly happens, whenever an Englishman, by perfidy or craft, kills an Irishman, however noble, or however innocent, be he clergy or layman, there is no penalty or correction enforced against the person who may be guilty of such wicked murder.

'But rather the more eminent the person killed and the higher rank which he holds among his own people, so much more is the murderer honoured and rewarded by the English, and not merely by the people at large, but also by the religious and bishops of the English race.'

This written plea had no effect on English policy and, rather than trusting in the power of the pen, native Irish clans resorted to the power of the sword.

This would have truly devastating consequences for the island, resulting in the eventual destruction of the ancient and noble Gaelic Order of clans such as the McKennas.

Chapter three:

Last stand

Discontent had grown on the island over the policy known as 'plantation', or settlement of loyal Protestants on lands held by the native Irish.

This policy had started during the reign from 1491 to 1547 of Henry VIII, whose Reformation effectively outlawed the established Roman Catholic faith throughout his dominions – and continued throughout the subsequent reigns of Elizabeth I, James I (James VI of Scotland), Charles I, and in the aftermath of the Cromwellian invasion of the island in 1649.

Rebellion erupted in 1594 against the increasingly harsh treatment of the native Irish and in the vanguard was the McKenna chieftain Patrick McKenna, Hugh O'Neill, 2nd Earl of Tyrone, and the O'Donnell chieftain Red Hugh O'Donnell.

In what became known as the Cogadh na Naoi mBliama, or the Nine Years War, they and their followers literally set the island ablaze in a vicious campaign of guerrilla warfare, wreaking a whirlwind of devastation on English settlements and garrisons in a daring series of lightning raids.

They inflicted a humiliating defeat on an English army at the battle of Clontibert in 1595, while in August of 1598 another significant defeat was inflicted at the battle of Yellow Ford.

As English control over Ireland teetered on the brink of collapse, thousands of more troops, including mercenaries, were hastily despatched to the island and, in the face of the overwhelming odds against them the rebel leaders, known as the Confederate Chiefs, sought help from England's enemy, Spain.

This arrived in the form of a Spanish invasion force that landed at Kinsale in 1601 under the command of Don Juan del Águila.

But, joined by part of the the rebel forces that included the McKennas, it was defeated following the siege of Kinsale, and Águila surrendered to Lord Mountjoy, Queen Elizabeth's Lord Deputy for Ireland.

Resistance continued until 1603, but proved abortive.

Three years later, in September of 1607 and in what is known as The Flight of the Earls, the 2nd Earl of Tyrone and the 1st Earl of Tyrconnel sailed into foreign exile from the village of Rathmullan, on the shore of Lough Swilly, in Co. Donegal, accompanied by ninety loyal followers.

Patrick McKenna died in 1612, by which time he had seen the almost complete destruction of the McKenna fortifications at Tully at the hands of Lord Mountjoy's troopers.

His grandson Niall, who succeeded him as the

McKenna chieftain, was also destined to play a formative role in one of the island's rebellions.

This was the insurrection that erupted in 1641 when at least 2,000 Protestant settlers were massacred at the hands of Catholic landowners and their native Irish peasantry, while thousands more were stripped of their belongings and driven from their lands to seek refuge where they could.

Terrible as the atrocities against the Protestant settlers were, subsequent accounts became greatly exaggerated, serving to fuel a burning desire on the part of Protestants for revenge.

The English Civil War intervened to prevent immediate action against the rebels, but following the execution of Charles I in 1649 and the consolidation of the power of England's Oliver Cromwell, the time was ripe for revenge.

The Lord Protector, as he was named, descended on Ireland at the head of a 20,000-strong army that landed at Ringford, near Dublin, in August of 1649, and the consequences of this Cromwellian conquest still resonate throughout the island today.

Cromwell had three main aims: to quash all forms of rebellion, to 'remove' all Catholic landowners who had taken part in the rebellion, and to convert the native Irish to the Protestant faith.

An early warning of the terrors that were in store for the Catholic Irish came when the northeastern town of

Drogheda was stormed and taken in September and between 2,000 and 4,000 of its inhabitants killed, including priests who were summarily put to the sword.

The defenders of Drogheda's St. Peter's Church, who had refused to surrender, were burned to death as they huddled for refuge in the steeple and the church was deliberately torched.

A similar fate awaited Wexford, on the southeast coast, where at least 1,500 of its inhabitants were slaughtered, including 200 defenceless women, despite their pathetic pleas for mercy.

Cromwell soon held the benighted land in a grip of iron, allowing him to implement what amounted to a policy of ethnic cleansing.

His troopers were given free rein to hunt down and kill priests, while Catholic estates such as those of the rebel McKennas were confiscated.

An estimated 11 million acres of land were taken and the dispossessed native Irish banished to Connacht and Co. Clare.

An edict was issued stating that any native Irish found east of the River Shannon after May 1, 1654 faced either summary execution or transportation to the West Indies.

The McKenna lands and fortifications at Tully were again devastated and Niall McKenna was forced to flee to Spain, where he later died.

Niall had been succeeded in the McKenna

chieftainship by his nephew, Phelemy McKenna who, along with his four sons, was murdered by English forces in 1666.

What proved to be the final death knell of families such as the McKennas was sounded in 1688 following what is known as the Glorious Revolution.

This involved the flight into exile of the Catholic monarch James II (James VII of Scotland) and the accession to the throne of the Protestant William of Orange and his wife Mary.

Followers of James were known as Jacobites, and prominent among them was Major John McKenna.

In the War of the Two Kings, or the Williamite War, Ireland became the battleground for an attempt by Jacobites to restore James to his throne – and in what is referred to as 'McKenna's Last Stand', or 'The Opening Shot of the Williamite Wars', Major McKenna led the Catholic Irish forces on behalf of James at the battle of Drumbanagher in March of 1688.

He was defeated and, refused terms of surrender, executed on the spot.

As a further act of callousness he was beheaded and his head despatched by the victorious Williamite troops to his widow.

One intriguing McKenna family legend is that when news of the disaster of the defeat at Drumbanagher reached his estate at Minmurray, the 'McKenna Treasure' was hastily dumped into the depths of Minmurray Lake – where it may lie to this very day.

Key events from the War of the Two Kings are marked annually in Northern Ireland – most notably the lifting of the siege of Derry, or Londonderry, by Williamite forces in 1689 and his victory at the battle of the Boyne the following year.

Final Jacobite defeat had been ratified through the signing of the Treaty of Limerick in 1691, under the terms of which many former rebels were allowed to seek a new life on foreign shores.

This set the pattern for waves of further emigration from Ireland, reaching its height in the wake of the Great Hunger of 1840 to 1848 when thousands starved to death because of a failure of the potato crop.

Born in 1771 in Clogher, Co. Tyrone, John MacKenna was among the many bearers of the name who established new lives for themselves far from the shores of their native land.

Immigrating to Spain where he trained as a military engineer, he later moved to what was then the Spanish Americas, serving as governor of the southern Chilean town of Osorno.

By this time known as Juan McKenna, he played a key role in Chile's fight for independence from Spain, later being commissioned by the first Chilean government to oversee the establishment of a new Chilean army.

Bitter struggles for power within the Chilean government later led to his exile to Argentina, where he was killed in a duel in 1814.

His grandson, Benjamin MacKenna, born in 1831 in Santiago, Chile, and who died in 1886, not only became a prominent Chilean politician but also a noted historian.

Chapter four:

On the world stage

Far from the destructive feuds of earlier centuries, McKennas have achieved distinction in a number of other endeavours.

Not only a prominent campaigner on behalf of wildlife but also a distinguished actress, **Virginia McKenna** was born in London in 1931.

Her screen debut after a successful career on stage came in 1952, winning a BAFTA Award for Best Actress for her role in *A Town Like Alice*, while six years later she received a Best Actress nomination for her performance in *Carve Her Name With Pride*.

She is best known for her role as Joy Adamson in the 1966 true-life film *Born Free*, with her husband Bill Travers co-starring beside her as her screen husband George Adamson.

The actress received a nomination for the Golden Globe Award for Best Actress in a Motion Picture, Drama, for her role, while the couple's experiences while filming – which focussed on the plight of the lioness Elsa – led to them becoming supporters of wild animal rights and for the protection of their natural habitats.

The actor and actress became involved in 1984 in the Zoo Check Campaign, while they set up the Born Free Foundation seven years later.

An Olivier Award for Best Actress in a British Musical came in 1979 for her performance opposite Yul Brynner in *The King and I*, while she was honoured with the O.B.E. in 2004 for her services to wildlife and the arts.

An equally distinguished actress on both stage and screen was the fluent Irish speaker **Siobhán McKenna**, born in 1923 in Belfast.

Raised much further south in Galway City, she joined an amateur Gaelic theatre group when aged in her teens, making her stage debut in 1940 in Galway's Gaelic Theatre.

Stage performances followed in Dublin's famed Abbey Theatre, while she made her debut on the Broadway stage in 1955 in *The Chalk Garden*, for which she received a Tony Award for Best Actress in a Leading Role, Drama.

She became so popular that she made the cover of Life magazine, appearing on screen in the 1961 *King of Kings*, the 1964 *Of Human Bondage*, and the 1965 *Dr. Zhivago*.

A proud Irishwoman, the actress was awarded before her death in 1986 with the Gold Medal of the Éire Society of Boston, Massachusetts, for 'having significantly fulfilled the ideals of the Éire Society, in particular spreading awareness of the cultural achievements of the Irish people.'

Also on the stage **Patrick McKenna**, born in 1960 in Hamilton, Ontario, is the Canadian actor who plays both dramatic and comedic roles and is best known for his appearances in the Canadian television series *The Red Green Show* and *Traders*.

He has also guest-starred in *Stargate SG-1*.

Behind the camera lens **David McKenna** is the American screenwriter and producer born in 1968 in San Diego, California, who is best known for writing *American History X*.

Born in 1944, **Bernard McKenna** is the Scottish writer and producer who has been involved in several top British television sitcoms, including *Doctor in the House*, *Robin's Nest*, *Shelley* and, from 1987 to 1994, *The New Statesman*.

He was also a collaborator of Graham Chapman, famed for his work on *Monty Python*, and of the late Peter Cook of Pete and Dud fame.

Listed as one of Britain's best-selling non-fiction authors, **Paul McKenna** is the hypnotist and television personality born in 1963 in Enfield, Middlesex.

It was not until the mid-1980s that he began to take an interest in hypnotism, after working as a radio broadcaster on stations that included BBC's Radio One.

In addition to entertaining audiences with his hypnotic skills, he is the author of a number of hypnosis-related books that include *I Can Make You Rich* and *Change Your Life in Seven Days*.

In the world of music **Barney McKenna** is the Irish musician who was born in 1939 in Donnycarney, Dublin.

Although a player of both the mandolin and the melodeon, he is so famed for his skills on the banjo that he is more popularly known as Banjo Barney.

A member of the band of traditional Irish musicians known as The Dubliners, he also played for a time with The Chieftains.

Bearers of the McKenna name have also stamped their mark on the world of politics.

Serving with the Union Army during the American Civil War, **Bernard J. McKenna**, born in Pittsburgh in 1842, returned to his native city to work in its booming iron industry.

Following a stint as a labour union official he was elected to the city council in 1875 and served as mayor from 1893 to 1896. He died in 1903.

Born in 1843 in Philadelphia, **Joseph McKenna** was the American politician who held the rare distinction of having served in all three branches of the U.S. Federal Government.

The son of Irish immigrants to America, he served in the House of Representatives from 1885 until 1897 when he was appointed Attorney General of the United States.

He served in this post until 1898 when he was appointed an Associate Justice of the Supreme Court, serving there until a year before his death in 1926.

Winning a seat in the Legislative Assembly of New Brunswick in 1982, **Frank McKenna**, born in 1948 in Apohaqui, New Brunswick, went on to become leader of the provincial Liberals in 1985.

It was under him that the Liberals won one of the largest election victories in Canadian history two years later, taking every seat in the legislature.

Serving as Premier of New Brunswick from 1987 to 1997, he later served from 2005 to 2006 as Canadian Ambassador to the United States.

Now retired from politics he is, at the time of writing, deputy chairman of the Toronto-Dominion Bank.

Over the ocean to Ireland, **Patricia McKenna**, born in 1957 in Castleshane, is the politician who in 1994 became the first Irish Green Party candidate to be elected to the European Parliament.

In the highly competitive world of sport **Sean McKenna**, born in 1962 in Quebec, is the former professional ice hockey forward who played for teams that include the Buffalo Sabres, Los Angeles Sabres, and Toronto Maple Leafs, while in the world of football **Kevin McKenna** is the player who, at the time of writing, plays for I.F.C. Koln in the German league.

Born in 1980 in Calgary, he also played from 2001 to 2002 with Scottish Premier League team Hearts, becoming the club's second highest goal scorer for that season – while he has also, at the time of writing, scored nine times in 36 appearances for the Canadian national team.

Established in 1924 through a donation by the Most Reverend Dr. McKenna, the **Dr. McKenna Cup**, known since 2008 as The Gaelic Life McKenna Cup, is a leading

Gaelic football competition played annually between the universities and the six counties of Ulster.

In the world of literature **John McKenna** is the Irish playwright and novelist who was born in 1952 and whose novels include *Clare*, *The Last Fine Summer*, and *A Haunted Heart*, while **Richard McKenna** was a former American sailor turned short-story writer and novelist.

Born in 1913 in Mountain Home, Idaho, he served in the U.S. Navy from 1931 until 1953 and turned his hand to writing after studying creative writing.

His 1962 novel *The Sand Pebbles* was adapted for the screen in 1996 for the film of the same name, while his science fiction work won him a Hugo Award for his short story *The Secret Place* – published posthumously following his death in 1964.

A writer, philosopher, and expert on the properties of plants, **Terence McKenna**, born in 1946 and who died in 2002, was the American author who explored the relationship between hallucinogenic drugs derived from plants and their effects down through the ages on human consciousness.

One of his best-known works is his 1992 *Food of the Gods: A Radical History of Plants, Drugs, and Human Evolution*.

Key dates in Ireland's history from the first settlers to the formation of the Irish Republic:

circa 7000 B.C.	Arrival and settlement of Stone Age people.
circa 3000 B.C.	Arrival of settlers of New Stone Age period.
circa 600 B.C.	First arrival of the Celts.
200 A.D.	Establishment of Hill of Tara, Co. Meath, as seat of the High Kings.
circa 432 A.D.	Christian mission of St. Patrick.
800-920 A.D.	Invasion and subsequent settlement of Vikings.
1002 A.D.	Brian Boru recognised as High King.
1014	Brian Boru killed at battle of Clontarf.
1169-1170	Cambro-Norman invasion of the island.
1171	Henry II claims Ireland for the English Crown.
1366	Statutes of Kilkenny ban marriage between native Irish and English.
1529-1536	England's Henry VIII embarks on religious Reformation.
1536	Earl of Kildare rebels against the Crown.
1541	Henry VIII declared King of Ireland.
1558	Accession to English throne of Elizabeth I.
1565	Battle of Affane.
1569-1573	First Desmond Rebellion.
1579-1583	Second Desmond Rebellion.
1594-1603	Nine Years War.
1606	Plantation' of Scottish and English settlers.
1607	Flight of the Earls.
1632-1636	Annals of the Four Masters compiled.
1641	Rebellion over policy of plantation and other grievances.
1649	Beginning of Cromwellian conquest.
1688	Flight into exile in France of Catholic Stuart monarch James II as Protestant Prince William of Orange invited to take throne of England along with his wife, Mary.
1689	William and Mary enthroned as joint monarchs; siege of Derry.
1690	Jacobite forces of James defeated by William at battle of the Boyne (July) and Dublin taken.

1691	Athlone taken by William; Jacobite defeats follow at Aughrim, Galway, and Limerick; conflict ends with Treaty of Limerick (October) and Irish officers allowed to leave for France.
1695	Penal laws introduced to restrict rights of Catholics; banishment of Catholic clergy.
1704	Laws introduced constricting rights of Catholics in landholding and public office.
1728	Franchise removed from Catholics.
1791	Foundation of United Irishmen republican movement.
1796	French invasion force lands in Bantry Bay.
1798	Defeat of Rising in Wexford and death of United Irishmen leaders Wolfe Tone and Lord Edward Fitzgerald.
1800	Act of Union between England and Ireland.
1803	Dublin Rising under Robert Emmet.
1829	Catholics allowed to sit in Parliament.
1845-1849	The Great Hunger: thousands starve to death as potato crop fails and thousands more emigrate.
1856	Phoenix Society founded.
1858	Irish Republican Brotherhood established.
1873	Foundation of Home Rule League.
1893	Foundation of Gaelic League.
1904	Foundation of Irish Reform Association.
1913	Dublin strikes and lockout.
1916	Easter Rising in Dublin and proclamation of an Irish Republic.
1917	Irish Parliament formed after Sinn Fein election victory.
1919-1921	War between Irish Republican Army and British Army.
1922	Irish Free State founded, while six northern counties remain part of United Kingdom as Northern Ireland, or Ulster; civil war up until 1923 between rival republican groups.
1949	Foundation of Irish Republic after all remaining constitutional links with Britain are severed.